I0006980

The Cryptocurrency - Blockchain Connection

Cryptocurrencies Are Not The Blockchain
Learn The Differences & Connections

Wayne Walker

Table of Contents

Introduction

Congratulations on your personal copy of *The Cryptocurrency-Blockchain Connection.* This special book will give you a foundation of cryptocurrencies and blockchain technology along with the ability to tell the difference. You will be exposed in great detail to the many, many possibilities of blockchain along with the limitations. Thanks for choosing this book!

The Next Level

Of Cryptocurrency Investing

Cryptocurrencies

(besides Bitcoin): What Do They Do?

For the many people that are still in awe of the amazing price movements upwards that we have seen across a lot of the cryptocurrencies, the one question that I receive the most from new students and others is "what do they do?" Bitcoin of course gets the spotlight, but for the other cryptos most people draw a blank. Let us have a look at the more popular coins and later some thoughts on the market movements.

Ethereum (ETH) - Programmable contracts

Bitcoin (BTC) - Moving money, settling transactions, a digital asset

Dash (DASH) - Key feature is privacy

Monero (XMR) - Private digital cash

Litecoin (LTC) - Similar to Bitcoin but faster

Ripple (XRP) - Enterprise payment settlement network

NEO (NEO) - Ethereum for the Chinese market

Why Have They Appreciated So Much?

Besides the questions about what purpose do cryptocurrencies serve, the next hottest topic is about the market movements. The story that I share often in class is about when I traveled to New York City in May of 2017 on a working vacation. Then, Bitcoin was trading at a little over $2,200, I returned to Europe in August and it was over $4,000. Now what was fundamentally different about Bitcoin by August to warrant an almost doubling in price? On the surface not much, however, Bitcoin and cryptocurrencies in general, are based on trust in the systems that supports them. With that in mind, the rocketing of Bitcoin beyond $19,000 and altcoins making eye-popping gains, for anyone setting a limit on what "is reasonable" is clearly indulging in wishful thinking. There is no exact science or logic here.

How You Should Trade Them

From my background and training within the capital markets, forex specifically, many of the coins are in extreme overbought territory. From some of the reports that I have read from different analysts, Bitcoin will continue to make massive gains. I can't really laugh at them anymore or apply all of my previous training. What can be used, and I strongly suggest this for anyone trading any asset class is to "make failure survivable" not my quote, it is well known to engineers and people involved with startups. Invest or trade with risk capital across several of the coins that have sufficient volume so that your ability to enter and exit is relatively easy. I am aware there are many views on what is sufficient volume, I need to see at least a 1,000,000 plus. Finally, you can also consider cryptos as a hedge to your investments or trading. They qualify because as an asset class they do not correlate with other assets for example stocks or commodities. In the later chapters we will explore deeper into the best trading practices for crypto trading.

After All the hype

What Should You Really Have in Your Crypto Portfolio?

For even the casual observer the fall of 2017 into the first two quarters of 2018 have been a wild ride in cryptocurrencies. It appears for now, as I had written in articles on the web, some of the hype would subside and we can get on with real crypto trading and investing. Actually, a lot of what I wrote (less hype, more regulations) has come true.

It is not with an "I told you so" attitude that I write the hype is taking a vacation, I write because the hype needed a vacation for the long term good of cryptocurrencies. I am well aware many people have been burned and their accounts have taken a few knockout blows. To be honest some have given up on cryptos all together. The majority of the departing crypto traders are those who refused or neglected to get some training or qualified advice before diving in. I have stressed in my other books the importance of diversification. An important concept with all asset classes but with cryptos it goes from good to have to MUST HAVE. This diversification concept is nothing magical or some deep secret. Just having knowledge of basic trading principles along with technical analysis would have helped many with their strategy and especially their mind-set.

The Reality

The fact is that the volatility we have seen with Bitcoin has actually been more severe in the past. Cryptos like other markets can actually go down, this point seemed like a new idea to some. When we were having the run up with Bitcoin from $10,000 to over $19,000 faster than even the biggest fan could have imagined, the downside was forgotten. The reduction in hype has helped to mature the market and it has also forced traders to have a more strategic look at the sector. Another plus, the Bitcoin sell off has had the benefit of allowing several altcoins to step into the limelight, for example Stellar.

The Portfolio

What I would consider to include in a 2018 and beyond portfolio:

Bitcoin, Ethereum, Ripple, Cardano, Stellar, NEO, Litecoin, EOS, and Nem. They are selected from my principle that investors or traders should have a diverse portfolio of cryptos and only trade those with good liquidity (by crypto standards). All the selected are in the top 15 in terms of market capitalization.

Both the new and more experienced crypto enthusiast should be aware of the unique features of the individual coin. Each crypto asset has its distinct features in terms of market behavior. We have also seen that altcoins have their own price movement stories. It is not so simple to say, as was said in the past, that whatever Ethereum or Bitcoin does in the market the others coins will react with similar price movements. For example, the decline in Bitcoin did not lead to an equivalent drop for many altcoins. To the contrary, several have increased in value.

ICOs

Outside of my list of suggested coins there can also be room for the speculative ICO or two. This is considered with the knowledge that many, but NOT all, are scams. Once you have selected your cryptos, the next step to further diversify the portfolio is to ensure that you have the appropriate sector mix. The majority of investors miss this critical detail when assembling a portfolio.

Take Your Crypto Portfolio
Diversification to the Next Level

Serious investors are usually on board with the idea that diversity is desirable in a portfolio. Whether one is trading typically secure government bonds to volatile cryptocurrencies, diversity is one thing that we can all agree on. This is especially true when it is common knowledge that roughly a 1,000 persons own 40 percent of the Bitcoin market, the so-called "Bitcoin whales." The whales, by the way, are in other coins as well.

What I will do is expand on the concept and share more of the strategies that high-net-worth crypto investors use with their portfolios. As I have covered in some of my articles, you should aim to have a portfolio with a mix of cryptos to avoid the madness of having all your money in Bitcoin or Ethereum. To first step to noticeably increase your diversification is to diversify by sector, as in the feature, and or main purpose of the coin.

Crypto Diversity By Sector

Some of the sectors to begin with: Tokens, Conventional, Smart Contracts, Settlement Networks, Privacy, Overlay Service. The suggestions listed are just that, suggestions. This is obviously not a complete list of every coin from every sector. The list however is a good starting point when assembling your portfolio.

The sectors and possible coins

Token: Stratus, EOS

Smart Contracts: NEO, Ethereum, Cardano

Privacy: Monero, Dash, Zcoin

Conventional: Litecoin, IOTA, NEM

Settlement Networks: Stellar, Ripple

Crypto Diversity By Exchanges

Diversity of exchanges is often overlooked in the risk management process. This oversight was especially painful in 2017 when several of the most well-known exchanges in the East and West had issues dealing with the market rush. These issues took the form of: servers being overloaded, sites were down, and for many the most painful was being unable to remove profits. This is a 24/7 market and major moves can come at any time, therefore the ability to execute is paramount. You begin the process by carefully selecting according to a mix of factors including: if regulated or not, the country, speed of bank transfers, market reputation, etc.

Extending the Head Start

Just by incorporating the diversity of exchanges steps, you will have a clear head start on many investors. To extend your head start, the next step is to consider the weight of each sector or coin in your portfolio. For example, if you have 4 coins in a sector do they each get 25% allocation of your funds or if 4 sectors do they each receive 25%? The final composition takes into account many factors, for example, your risk tolerance, your exposure to other asset classes, and the size of your account. These are some of the things that I work on with clients to help them have a piece of mind.

You then continue the process by seeing what percentage of funds are with each exchange. The crypto market remains mostly unregulated, if your exchange goes bust there is very little help to get from any government, therefore being aware of what percentage of funds are sitting with each exchange is a necessary part of your risk management.

Traps To Avoid When Making the Transition

From Forex to Cryptocurrency Trading

How to transition successfully from forex to cryptocurrency is a challenge for many traders. Much of what I will share is based mostly on my experience with the transition to cryptocurrencies. Therefore, it is by no means the only way.

The first thing to be aware of is that a lot of what you know from trading spot forex can be applied to cryptocurrency, but there are some crucial differences. These differences, if ignored, can be fatal to your account.

The most important fact that forex traders must come to terms with is that they are not dealing with fiat currencies like the Euro or the US Dollar. Cryptocurrencies are not legal tender in any country, they are not currencies in the traditional sense. To put it another way, if you go to your local coffee shop they are not required to accept Bitcoin as payment. Now, if the coffee shop were in Madrid and you had Euros they would have to accept them because the Euro is legal tender in Spain. Cryptos are also subject to the regulatory whims of a government. A country, with little warning, could ban a crypto or a crypto exchange. This, on the other hand is not an everyday risk with fiat currencies. It is extremely unlikely that you will wake up tomorrow to a headline "US Dollar trading has been banned in the US" or "New York State has declared it illegal for residents to trade on NYSE."

The other issue that we are dealing with is technology. Cryptos can be programmed and I am unaware of any programmable fiats. We have also discovered with several of the cryptos that they have not been able to live up to their stated or promised capabilities. This doesn't even include the cases where there was outright fraud.

New Rules for News Trading

The normal strategies of foreign currency economic news trading do not directly apply. For example, a Non-Farm Payrolls jobs report or a Bank of England interest rate announcement will have little to no impact on Litecoin. However, your experience of dealing with reactions to news can be applied to cryptos, for example, a concept familiar to many forex traders is market overreaction to news. Overreaction to news is almost a cliché in cryptocurrency trading because most traders are both new and unfamiliar with market volatility. In addition, you have thought-paralyzing levels of madness that have me scratching my head when I hear the stories of people who have maxed out credit cards just to buy Bitcoins. If I were in a situation like that I guess I would be overreacting too.

Technical Analysis With 25,000% Returns

On the technical analysis front a lot of what you should already know about support and resistance is useful. What is new is that you will need to suspend strict interpretation of support/resistance levels. You have cryptos that can easily jump 100% per month and with many technical indicators this would be considered massively overbought, however, with cryptos a certain amount of suspension of disbelief is needed. Some proof, Pantera Bitcoin Fund returned over 25,000% (launched in 2013) or Ripple with 35,000% return for 2017. Not typos, both are easily verifiable with a simple Google search. The best way to deal with movements like these is to acknowledge that what is going on is not supposed to, but it is. As I have written before, we are in a new crypto universe that is expanding and changing with each day. Today what is legal can be suddenly illegal tomorrow. What you read and assumed to be true in the morning, can turn out to be "fake news" by lunch.

The whales of Bitcoin and cryptos in general are a real factor to deal with. As mentioned earlier they control more or less 40 percent of the market. This is unheard of in any other asset class. These whales depending on their mood can destroy your weeks of carefully planned analysis and strategy.

The entry of the institutional market players for example, Goldman Sachs and others will bring "smart" money to the market but especially liquidity. When they enter the market with huge amounts of capital this signals to other market players that cryptocurrencies are something to be taken seriously. Overall this is better for traders in general as it will help to mature the market along with the other mentioned benefits.

New York Stock Exchange (NYSE) has signaled in early 2018 that they are investigating the launch of a platform that will allow institutional clients to trade and store Bitcoins. This news alone could signal and form the basis of further price appreciation of Bitcoin and cryptos in general for the long term.

Death of the Purist

Being a fundamental or technical analysis purist will only leave you with an underperforming account. Therefore you will need a robust risk management strategy using many of the tools that should be familiar to you. You manage the risk by having as a foundation my non-negotiable rule of being able to survive failure, which means only trade what you can afford to lose. From there you add a diverse portfolio of cryptos and only trade those with good liquidity.

Crypto Exchanges:

Front-running and Pricing

Dealing with exchanges is a part of trading and with cryptos there are some issues that many investors are unaware of. The positive is that with the 24/7 market you can trade whenever it pleases you. The unpleasant reality is the front-running of your trades by the exchanges. Front-running is when a broker enters a trade ahead of its clients', usually done before a big trade that will likely influence the price of a crypto, stock, etc. This is both unethical and illegal in the regulated markets. Much of the crypto world is unregulated therefore exchanges have room to play. It is common knowledge that this practice is widespread in the market. For the most part, it is done with decent size trades because there is more of an incentive to profit from the front-running. If you are trading micro amounts of Bitcoin it really should not affect you.

Pricing and Spreads

The other hot topic with exchanges is pricing. Typically, on regulated exchanges, for example with stocks, you will usually get the best bid and ask prices. This is far more difficult to achieve with the crypto markets because the supply is so fragmented. The actual price that you will be executed on varies widely by the exchange that you use as a trading partner. One of the important variables includes how robust is the matching engine that they use. A trade matching engine is the software used by electronic exchanges, it matches up bids and offers to complete trades. Algorithms are used to execute the allocation. In addition to the two main issues that I covered, you could also run into latency problems if you are running an algorithm.

A spread is the difference between the buy and sell price. The spreads for cryptos when compared to other markets are huge. So huge that it was one of the hottest areas of complaints at the crypto trader event that I attended recently in New York City. As we have seen with other markets, the expectation is that the spreads will decrease with time.

None of this is meant to be an exchange bashing exercise, but instead an alert for traders. This is especially important for new traders and investors whom are often unaware of what they are dealing with when placing a trade. Exchanges do serve an important role in the market and remember that the cryptocurrency world remains relatively new and there is plenty of room to improve.

Security for
Your Account

With cryptos most of the responsibility for security rest with you, the individual user. If you choose to use an exchange they will play their role but in the end you are responsible. One of the reasons why security is such a big issue with blockchain transactions is that they are immutable and cannot be cancelled once done. For example, you send funds to another party by mistake, unless they feel like returning it, you should consider the funds lost. This is a benefit and risk of cryptocurrencies.

Why is There a Need for a Whole Chapter on Security?

Over $1billion has been stolen in cryptocurrencies within the past few years. The biggest theft was at Coincheck, 2018, with a loss of $500M, the well-known Mt. Gox 2014, had an estimated loss of $480M, and Parity Wallet 2017, an estimated loss of $155M. This is just a sample and I have only included _known_ thefts.

Some of the Common Attack Patterns

- Phishing: user details including 2FA (Two factor Authentication) are stolen on a fake site typically by email. The details are later entered into the real site after being captured from the fake one.

- Key logging viruses track user credentials when they log in and then compromises the account

- Copy and paste viruses hijack your paste function causing you to enter an attacker's address when transferring funds

- ICO sites have been copied and replaced by scammers, therefore be extra careful when participating in ICOs. Verify they are legitimate.

Medium to Advanced Security Practices

- Do not get phished. Never click a link and login from an email

- Do not use your regular email for your crypto trading account

- Always use Two factor Authentication for all

- Use different emails for each cryptocurrency exchange

- Use a trusted antivirus software and avoid questionable sites that may compromise your computer

- Remove the coins that you do not plan to trade in the short-term from the exchange

- Use a separate computer that is only used for crypto trading

- Keep as many coins as possible in a hardware wallet

- Wallets apps on your computer are good, but back up the private keys

Cryptojacking?

This is one of the newer forms of crypto misconduct. It involves the use of a computer to mine cryptocurrencies without the owner's permission. To be more direct, your computer is hijacked to work on someone's crypto mining.

The bad guys or girls execute the scheme by loading a program on your computer through the browser when visiting some compromised site. Shortly after, your machine begins solving computational problems that generate cryptocurrency mining rewards for the crypto-jackers. As you can imagine they will not share their rewards with you.

Your Defense

Keep a close eye on your computer's task manager. There are several browser extensions that will help your security efforts, one of them is MinerBlock from the Chrome web store. It blocks browser-based cryptocurrency miners.

The New World
of Government-Backed Cryptocurrencies

It did not take long for the cryptocurrency fever to begin infecting governments around the world. Several of them have recently announced their intentions to issue their own cryptocurrencies. This is an astonishing turnaround from those who on the surface might have an interest in stifling the spread of cryptocurrencies.

The Landscape

Venezuela has launched their cryptocurrency backed by the resources of the country, which mainly consists of oil and gas. It is called Petro and it mimics some of the features of Bitcoin. Venezuela, as many people know is suffering from a long list of economic ills. The American sanctions have not helped the situation and President Nicolás Maduro has made no attempt to conceal his goal that this Petro cryptocurrency will provide a new way of circumventing them.

Russia also announced their goal of introducing a crypto Ruble. The goal is similar to that of Venezuela, which is to navigate around current or future sanctions. Russia, however is not in the same economic emergency as Venezuela. From what I have researched and heard they have a more let us wait and see attitude, in contrast to Venezuela which has already launched.

Not to be left out, even the Bank of England (BOE) recently revealed they are exploring the option of their own BOE backed crypto. I can only imagine that many other central banks are also investigating the possibility of their own digital currencies.

The Reaction

The general attitude in the crypto universe and mine is that this journey forward has several ideological and practical barriers. The most obvious is that if these government cryptos are truly intended to replace Bitcoin or any cryptocurrency, they would contradict some of the most central features of the crypto world, which is having a permissionless and decentralized ledger. Permissionless is especially non-negotiable for cryptocurrency enthusiasts. This alone will have the sides clashing because one of the things governments find irresistible is the taste of control. In essence, with these state-backed cryptocurrencies they are playing digital dress up with their fiat currency. You don't like the Euro? No problem, we have it for you now in crypto format. They changed the name and packaging, but the DNA of government control remains. Many have mentioned another obvious, if the system gets hacked (we can pretty much guarantee there will be constant attempts) who covers the losses? Are governments ready to begin paying compensation once the Pandora's box of state-backed cryptocurrencies opens?

The Launch

Since the Petro coin 2018 second quarter release market players have had their eyes on Venezuela. The market reception so far has been mixed but it is still too early to pass a final verdict. The hackers I am sure were also eager for the launch. My advice to the Venezuelan government, if they are open to my suggestions, "make failure survivable." From a cryptocurrency purist point of view, any centralized cryptocurrency is playing dress up and a non-starter.

What to Expect with

Cryptocurrencies in the Near Future

These are purposely short-term expectations, because in my view, making long-term claims about cryptos is a fool's errand. We are in the very early stages in a shift from a total, once unquestioned, belief in government issued currencies into the potential that cryptocurrencies have to offer us. Just as with fiat currencies, belief and trust in the system in essential. The almost unbelievable gains that many of the cryptos have experienced is a mix of many factors including, news, speculators, and the value proposition of the individual coins. I would further claim that the increasing trust by the general public and the institutional finance sector is the major factor. For example, in 2017 the French firm Tobam launched the first Bitcoin mutual fund in Europe. Trust being what it is, it can change, therefore buckle up! Because for all the 900% plus gains, the market can easily produce just as dramatic drops if negative issues regarding trust reappear within the cryptocurrency ecosystem.

Less ICO Madness

The ICO madness will lose some of the irrational gold rush mentality and we will see improved self-policing from the current players in the market. We are already seeing a crackdown by regulators in the United States, Europe and elsewhere. The public and government regulators do have limits on what they will tolerate. We are also seeing more; search, identify, and prosecute missions from authorities globally on the ICO swindlers. This is great news for most people, the scammers are obviously unhappy.

More Regulations

I was recently made aware of the amount of agencies that claim jurisdiction over cryptocurrencies. This is just in the United States alone, you have the Treasury Department's FinCEN, the Securities and Exchange Commission, and the Internal Revenue Service. The story gets more bizarre, because there is not even agreement among the regulators on what Bitcoin is. For example, the IRS treats it as property and the Commodity Futures Trading Commission says it is a commodity. For market participants this bring confusion to new levels. Even with the confusion, to increase the trust of the broader retail and institutional markets, there is a need of more appropriate regulations for this growing market. This should also include swift and robust punishment for those engaging in misconduct.

With the regulations, you will often find there is a pattern that follows market innovations like cryptos. First, we have the Wild West, followed by overregulation to calm the public. Later the cooler heads prevail and there is a rollback of some rules and finally ending with a workable balance.

Expanded Practical Application of Cryptos

Myth number one and in my opinion the biggest about cryptos, is that they have no practical applications. The reality is that several of the major coins have real life applications and are related to improving existing sectors in the market. Legacy firms that push this "no practical applications" myth are rarely happy about innovations that did not come from themselves and are quick to discredit any challengers.

In January 2018 the money transfer firm MoneyGram agreed to test Ripple due to its speed with executing transactions. Ripple was designed to speed up money transfers and international transactions. It reduces both the money transfer time and costs. Since it was only a test we will need to wait for the final results but it clearly proves there are real-world applications.

Another example includes when Ethereum was used to execute a real estate transaction. It became news when the founder of TechCrunch used it and a smart contract* to buy an apartment in the Ukraine without the need of travelling to the country.

*Smart Contracts: can manage agreements between people, executing the terms of a contract when the mutually agreed upon terms and conditions are met.

Greater use of Cryptocurrencies in the Emerging Markets

We will likely see the continued spread of cryptocurrencies in the emerging markets. This is because cryptos are not controlled by any country or directly tied to any government's legal tender. The practical application of this means if a shaky government collapses, the value of a cryptocurrency like Bitcoin in most cases will be untouched. This benefit may seem unnecessary to your average developed western country, but in unstable countries the decentralization feature of cryptos has a *very* real and practical use.

Waiting to see more of

What I am eagerly awaiting to see more of in the near crypto future.

1-Exchanges will upgrade both security and their capacity to deal with demand surges. Even though crypto exchanges are not subjected to the same level of scrutiny as traditional exchanges, going forward this security issue will become increasingly difficult to keep talking around. Why? the crypto landscape has enough sad tales of hackings with millions being stolen. No region in the world gets to point fingers. It happens in the East and it also happens in the West, to both big and small exchanges. In contrast to funds in your local bank, if your account is hacked at an exchange, there is very little recourse to recovering your funds and as of this writing there is no insurance available. Everyone knows hackers are on a dedicated hunt after cryptocurrency accounts, therefore the defense needs to step up. The internal threats are another set of headaches, they range from insider trading to other financial misconduct from employees.

Several of the regulated and larger exchanges buckled under the demand for new accounts during the recent market explosions. They will get a pass this time around, but how many more times will the public or those in power remain so forgiving?

2- Autumn 2017 saw the launch of Bitcoin futures and it will be interesting to see how this plays out. The public has been asking for a more regulated market, well trading on a futures exchange is all about regulations. This was also the first time that Bitcoin traders could hedge their positions in a regulated market. They now have the ability to take the other side in the market by shorting.

3- More coins that eliminates the need for miners. Currently, the majority of Bitcoin mining is done by a handful of firms. Not a market healthy situation as they can use this influence in undesirable ways.

4- Improvements in the speed of Bitcoin transactions seems to be catching the attention of many industry influencers. Even for Bitcoin fans, the relatively slow pace of a routine transaction can be an issue. There are several cryptos that are taking on these challenges and I am excited to see how this develops.

Bitcoin and Altcoin Trading

Cryptos provide volatility, as traders we love this, it is sweet music for us. Why? If you place a trade and nothing happens then you have just paid the spread to your broker for nothing. Trading is a business (or you should treat it as one), for you to recover your cost of the transaction (the spread) you need and want volatility.

Rumors and panics add to the volatility. There can also be extreme sensitivity to news, 20% daily moves are **not** uncommon. The autumn of 2017, even by crypto standards, the volatility that we saw was astonishing.

Advantages

There are usually no trade size minimums, in contrast to trading stocks, commodities, or spot forex. You can also short sell, therefore an up or a down market are both okay with you. Other advantages are that you have the ability to trade directly with the exchanges, brokers are not mandatory. You can trade 24/7 which is even more trading hours than spot forex. Obviously, the liquidity is not equal throughout the day, some times of the day are more liquid than others.

Day Trading

Day trade with caution! For now you are trading mostly against inexperienced traders, but the scene is changing. The autumn of 2017 saw the launch of Europe's first Bitcoin mutual fund in France. There are also reports of several hedge and private funds with huge resources prepping to enter the market.

Market Timing

Getting in at the "perfect time" with Bitcoin and cryptocurrencies is unrealistic. What is going on, weekly double digits gains, is not supposed to, but it is. Using strictly technical analysis or fundamentals will fail you. Look to buy on panic drops, bounces upwards after Bitcoin panic drops have been very profitable. One tactic to deal with

44

the volatility is to have price alerts set for noticeable price moves. I strongly suggest that you accumulate gradually, cryptocurrency wealth takes time. Ignore, as much as possible, the Wild West hype going on. If your crypto position has a 100% + move up, take some profits. If you did not have an existing position, after a major breakout upwards, buy on the pullbacks. The best opportunities are there for the informed and less emotional. This is especially true in an arena with crypto traders who are untested with facing 40-50% drops.

Leverage

Leverage? Use with caution and only with entities that offer reliable stop losses. Bitcoin and cryptos in general, are assets that can move 20-30% (either direction) on some days, therefore your account can easily blow up. You lose money when you get taken out, and that can easily happen with high leverage. Bottom line, stay in the game and any long-term shorting is with extreme caution...keep in mind all the "deaths" of Bitcoin.

Trading Tactics

Here we will examine the major reasons why traders lose money and most important we will explore the solutions.

Unrealistic Expectations: It is important when getting into trading, as with many things, that one must have a realistic idea of what you are dealing with. Unrealistic expectations can take the form of someone starting with what is a mini-trader account of 1,000 or maybe 2,000 USD and expecting overnight riches.

You can even begin with 100 or 200 dollars, which is fine. There is nothing wrong with the amount, but those same traders at 100 or 200 dollars are expecting to have 1,000 or 2,000 dollars in their accounts within a couple days. There are firms out there that have actually mentioned or even promised them that they can do this. While I am not saying it is impossible, I am saying it is unrealistic. It is essential that you do have a sense of reality to your trading.

No Plan: Many people say "failing to plan is planning to fail", with planning, your trading is in alignment with your timeframe and the results that you are expecting to receive. A trading plan is essential, because without one you are setting yourself up for potentially huge losses. Without a plan there is no point in entering trading.

Too Much Risk: It could be the person with 100 dollars in their account or even 100,000. It is not the amount that is critical, but the amount you are risking in relation to the funds available. You begin from the position of making "failure survivable". This concept is based on the idea that your losses should not be catastrophic. For example, each position should not use more than 5 or 6% of your available risk capital. This will also mean that if leverage is used it should be a low amount.

Confusing Trading With Investing: In my years as a banker, I have had countless clients who I have had to repeatedly point out that they should not confuse the two. Trading is about making money short-term, it is income generating activity, you are moving in and out of trades. Investing is more long-term and usually has a minimum timeframe of a year. It could be that some of your investment goals are derived from your trading but do not confuse them. It may seem basic to some, but speaking from experience of advising clients globally there are still many out there that get trading and investment confused.

Solutions:

It's ok to talk about problems and challenges, but obviously we need to have some solutions.

Low Leverage: To avoid the problem of too much risk, a proven solution is using low leverage. You keep the leverage low because it gives you time to think, to react more effectively, and you are not as sensitive to changes in the market.

Scaling In Scaling Out: Scaling in scaling out is one of my favorites. I use it with investing and also with my trading. Scaling in scaling out, the theory behind it is that you allow the market to tell you which way to go, it is that simple. An example, I plan to buy 250 of GCMS altcoins after having done my technical and fundamental analysis. How to begin? I would start with a 25 or 50 coins position and allow the market to confirm if I am on the right path. If I bought GCMS coins at 100 dollars and they suddenly jump to 125 per coin, great, the market is confirming that I made the correct decision. In this example if I began with 25 coins, I would then add another 25 or 50 and repeat the process until I reach my goal of 250 coins.

There are some who might say I missed out a little on the move from 100 to 125 and I did somewhat, but I am also more secure in my decision by being patient. On the reverse, getting back to scaling out, let us imagine that the market had moved against me, instead of having 250 coins at risk initially, it would have been only 25. Obviously there is a trade off, but from experience, it is to the advantage of those who are scaling in scaling out.

Another example, let us say you bought 100 coins at 100 dollars each and the price suddenly drops to 90. What I would suggest, instead of selling everything immediately, that you consider selling only 25 or 30 because the drop could be due to an overreaction in the market. There are several things that could be at play, for example a false rumor, again you are allowing the market to guide you along the correct path. Of course if the price continues to fall then you decide on a final exit if it goes beyond your mental stop loss.

Trade Liquid Markets: To trade liquid markets is something I can't overemphasize. Having one, long shot type trade (with ultra-risk capital) is fine, as long as you are aware of the risk. However, for regular trading, the cryptos with low liquidity by cryptocurrency standards, are not my first choice. Liquidity is critical especially as a trader, an investor is not as time sensitive, but if you are trading where you might need to make sudden moves you want to be holding liquid cryptocurrencies.

Liquid, to be very clear, is the ability to move in and out of the trade with ease. Being in a trade and having paper profits is wonderful. However, when it is time to convert the paper profits into real ones and if you are unable to do so, then it is a bad joke as you can only watch them, not very nice. On the other side if you are in a loss and are unable to exit that position, it turns into a nightmare. I don't care who is giving tips, or whatever blog you are reading, you must trade liquid cryptocurrencies, there is no other way.

Selecting Cryptocurrencies: Select a few and get to know them well. As you can imagine no trader is trading 600 different coins at a time. A lot of people begin with cryptos by trading the most well-known ones, Bitcoin, Ethereum, for example. After a while, by trading a few selected cryptos they will become familiar to you and you will get a deeper sense of how they move.

Putting It All Together

Traders must have a system. We will examine and connect the different aspects of a trading system.

Trading Platform: Selecting your trading platform is important because the platform is the vehicle that you use to conduct trading. Since the trading is online it is essential that you are using a platform that matches your style. It could be one that is either multi-asset or one that is more basic. You should know the provider behind the platform. With cryptocurrencies you have the option of using either a trading platform or dealing directly with an exchange. New exchanges are regularly popping up on the market and depending on the country you will need to be careful. I suggest that you get a recommendation from a friend or a trusted crypto advisor.

Goals: Without goals it is really difficult to begin trading. The analogy that I have heard and like to use, in regards to goals, is that without one it would be the equivalent of heading to a railway ticket counter and just say "give me a ticket!" and of course they would ask "a ticket to where?"
Short-term goals could be monthly or weekly profit targets, they are individualized. Goals must match your style and the amount of risk capital available for trading.

Long-term goals are often related to your investment strategy. They are also related to your short-term goals because the long-term goals should be based on the short-term profit targets. There must be a matchup, because if you have a weekly target of 100 dollars and a monthly target of a 1,000 then there is a discrepancy that needs to be addressed.

Mental Preparation: You do need to be psychologically ready to trade. If you are about to trade and are tense or nervous, then you need to take time off. Go meditate, get some exercise, do something else, but it is important that you do not trade until you are psychologically ready.

With trading you must have the mindset of not taking things personally. Remove emotions from trading, the goal is simply to make money.

Know your risk tolerance: How much are you willing to risk on each trade? It is important, remember traders' golden rule number one, "no cash, no trading." It doesn't matter what anyone tells you, if there is no cash, there is no trading and this must be taken seriously. This ties in with your risk tolerance, for example, having a cash balance of 10,000 USD and you want to risk 1%, the amount is 100 dollars. Meaning that of your risk capital, regardless of what you are trading, when you set your stop loss (mental or on a platform) it should not exceed 100 USD.

Do your due diligence: A new day has begun and your computer is on, what happened overnight? What happened on the crypto markets? You should be aware of the news that came out overnight and more importantly how the markets reacted to it. Sometimes, what in theory should be good news, the markets can surprise with a negative reaction.

How to select your entry level: Knowing your entry points means you have a good reason for every trade that you execute. If you do not have a good reason, I suggest that you take the funds and turn them over to a charity. When selecting your entry level, you need a good risk-reward ratio and this should match your risk tolerance. Technical/fundamental analysis is also taken into consideration. The support and resistance levels, news, are all essential before you execute any trade. If you are trading cryptos you need to be aware of where the support and resistance lines are for the time frame that you are trading.

Know Your Exit Levels: What is your profit target, is it a thousand dollars or a few? You need to be aware of this. When you are setting stops to control losses, the first thing to do is to ensure that they fall within your parameters. Same as with your entry level, you should know the fundamental analysis, support and resistance levels, and another traders' golden rule "cut your losses and let profits run." Many traders say the profits take care of themselves but you must keep a close eye on the losses.

Keep a Journal: It may not be for everyone but it is something that I use to record my trading. It includes several things, where I entered the trade, my exit level, and why I thought the trade was a good idea when I entered it. In review of your journal, if there are patterns, you will begin to detect them. You can either remove a pattern that is not working or expand on one that is. This helps you to fine-tune your trades.

Review Your Results: Review your profit or loss for the day. It is important because while trading can be fun, it is a business and the point is to make a profit. If in the review of your profit/loss you discover it is not what you had intended, your duty is to find out why. You also need to know what was behind your good results. Maybe it was pure luck, and if that was the case, great, but luck is normally not a sustainable strategy for trading. I would suggest, as I do in my trading, review your journal. Was it market news? Or was it the size of the positions? These factors can influence the results.

Your Next Steps

Before diving in, you could also prepare some more with an online class, I have one at (gcmsonline.info) or simply speaking with a trusted advisor. I will caution about using some of the online crypto forums. Most are without any sort of real supervision. Just a scan of several of the large ones available on the main social media networks and the answers provided to some of the questions from members are absolutely scary.

The past few months have shaken the confidence of many about the crypto markets, especially those who bought in December of 2017 to only see their accounts implode. I have met a few in class and I will share with you what I told them along with some charts: if in for the long term, take a deep breath and let things play themselves out. A lot of what we are seeing has been seen before in the crypto markets.

Bitcoin and cryptocurrencies have travelled far from the days of when they were mostly associated with criminals. Now there is both a broader and more positive public awareness. Bitcoin futures transactions are even cleared by top name Wall Street firms, something that not along ago would have been laughed at. For progress to continue as I have explained, there needs to be less hype, more relevant regulations, and greater security plus transparency from the exchanges. These suggestions I believe will secure that cryptocurrencies as an asset class moves beyond the early adopters phase.

Blockchain

Real-World Applications And Understanding

Introduction

We depart from the world of cryptocurrencies and enter into the sphere of blockchains which is the underlying technology of cryptos. This section should greatly expand your knowledge of blockchains and their applications. It should equally increase your ability to separate the reality of the technology from much of the hype that we are experiencing in the market.

What is Blockchain?

In 2008 the first blockchain was designed by Satoshi Nakamoto who introduced the idea in a white paper with Bitcoin. Bitcoin was the first execution of the technology. Blockchain is a *type* of Distributed Ledger Technology (DLT). A distributed ledger is replicated, shared, and synchronized data geographically spread across sites, institutions, or countries. It is important to note from the beginning that *Distributed ledgers do not have a central administrator.* DLT is the underlying technology for Bitcoin and other cryptocurrencies.

A Different Tool for Different People

Cryptocurrencies are of least importance to a blockchain specialist because it does a lot more! As a matter of fact some blockchainers, as I like to call them, sometimes get annoyed when you bring up the topic of cryptocurrencies at their events.

For crypto enthusiasts, blockchain is the technical backbone of digital currencies. The developers use it for storing data on a distributed network and for the futurists it is a tool for creating a decentralized society.

Blockchain Building Blocks

Every block in a ledger is connected to the previous block by a cryptographic algorithm called a hash. The linked blocks form a chain, thus giving us the term "blockchain."

Blockchain is a form of database that is distributed, and operates on a consensus basis. The computers on the network, known as nodes, validate transactions and adds them to the blockchain. With no centralized source to verify changes, a distributed consensus algorithm is used to create agreement between nodes so that the same entry is made to each ledger.

64

Decentralization: Each party on a blockchain has access to the entire database and its complete history. Every party can validate the records of its partners without an intermediary.

Immutability: Each block has a timestamp and link to the previous block. The blocks are resistant to modifications. Once recorded, the data in any block cannot be altered retroactively without the alteration of all subsequent blocks. Algorithms are deployed to ensure the recording in the database is permanent.

Peer-2-Peer (P2P) Transmission: Communication occurs directly between peers without a central node.

Programmable: The transactions can be programmed. Users can set up algorithms and rules that automatically trigger transactions between nodes.

Let's Get Nerdy

A block contains data, its hash, and the hash of the previous block. Now let us get a little deeper in the explanation:

Data: The data stored depends on the type of block. For example with a cryptocurrency it might contain information on the sender, receiver, and the amount of the transaction.

Its hash: Once a block is created the hash is calculated. The hash is unique, basically it is the fingerprint for the block. It identifies both the block and its contents.

Hash: Hash of the previous block.

An example: Block 4 has its own hash, plus the hash of block 3. Only block 1 has no previous hash and this is known as the Genesis Block. If you alter the hash of block 3, all subsequent blocks are invalid because block 4 already has the correct hash of the previous block (block 3). Therefore all other bocks after 3 are invalid.

The distributed P2P network: If you alter the hash of block 3 when sent to the network it will be rejected by the other nodes (because it was altered).

To succeed with tampering, you must alter all the blocks. Redo the Proof-of-Work of each block to take control of 51% of the P2P network. *Proof-of-Work: Slows down the creation of new blocks.

Proof-of-Work: Is the most used method of establishing consensus. Proof-of-Work consensus requires each node to solve an extremely complex equation in order to complete each block. The point of the complexity of the equation is to force each node to use a significant amount of processing power and electricity in order to solve it. An expanded definition is provided in the "Blockchain First Aid" chapter later on in the book.

Types of Blockchains

The first is a permissionless or public blockchain, which means that anyone can access it. Next is a permissioned which is private. This is a closed network of nodes and only those relevant to the transactions can gain access. This is best for governments, hospitals, insurers, etc. There is also a hybrid blockchain where anyone can access it but not all can make updates. Another hybrid version could be some data is readable to the public, some of it is not.

Keep in Mind

Blockchain really shines best in low-trust environments. These are situations where participants are unable to deal directly with each other or lack a trusted intermediary.

Blockchain verifies but does NOT validate therefore, garbage in garbage out. False data could have been entered, this also applies to all off-chain data. It is only as strong as the weakest link, for example if sensors registering data are incorrect the blockchain is incorrect.

People also need to remember that lot of the technology involved is first world so it is not for everyone and it cannot solve all problems. The technology and human systems must be aligned.

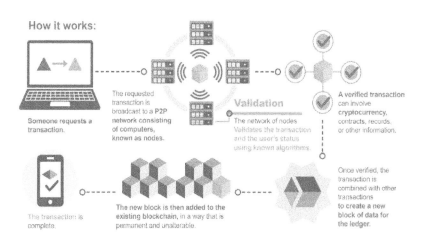

Figure 2: Blockchain and key features at a glance

How it works:

Someone requests a transaction.

The requested transaction is broadcast to a P2P network consisting of computers, known as nodes.

Validation
The network of nodes Validates the transaction and the user's status using known algorithms.

A verified transaction can involve cryptocurrency, contracts, records, or other information.

Once verified, the transaction is combined with other transactions to create a new block of data for the ledger.

The new block is then added to the existing blockchain, in a way that is permanent and unalterable.

The transaction is complete.

A Basic Blockhain Network

Do You Need Blockhain?

In my effort to reduce some of the unneeded hype around blockchain technology we will review the questions that must be answered before setting up a network.

Is the database being considered likely to be attacked or do you need redundant copies on multiple distributed computers? If yes, then there is possible need for a blockchain. If no, then there is no need for a blockchain.

Does more than one participant need to update the data? If yes, then possible need for a blockchain. However if they trust each other, then no. If they would trust a third party, also no.

Does the data need to be kept private? Yes, then a need for blockchain.

Do you need to control who can make changes to the blockchain? If yes, you might need a permissioned blockchain.

A no answer to the previous two questions leads to a possible need of a public blockchain.

Before Getting on the Blockchain Train

Before launching a blockchain project, you should investigate if your or some traditional database technology can meet your needs. It is essential to clarify if the problem requires blockchain technology instead of going blockchain and then attempting to see if you have any use for it.

Any business case for blockchain must also account for the potential costs beyond hosting, licensing, and implementation. Much of the dramatic cost saving predictions, especially in the finance sector with replacing legacy systems is unlikely at the levels predicted. The hype often fails to sufficiently account for future costs in power and storage. Energy expenses may increase significantly as transactions volume goes up. The increased storage costs are because each node must maintain a ledger of all transactions from the beginning of the blockchain. Along with the technical aspects, employee education on blockchain and the practical adaptations must be included in the strategy.

Investment in
Blockchain by Sectors

Blockchain remains a relatively young technology. Most of the short-term value will be in cost reduction. The hospitality, automotive, and financial services are some of the early adopters. In the financial services alone, so far 90 plus major banks in the United States, Canada and Europe are *already* testing blockchain solutions.

Some of the biggest finance names like Citi and Bank of America are busy securing patents to capture certain segments of the market. The segments include wire transfers, payment systems, and even their own cryptocurrencies.

Practical Applications and Real World Use

- New York Interactive Advertising Exchange (NYIAX): Is using blockchain as a way to provide an ads marketplace for publishers.

- Maersk: Has blockchain based projects for maritime logistics to explore potential cost savings. This is due to the expense of verifying freight documents which is sometimes more costly than the shipping. This expensive process involves over 200 persons that includes agents, government officials, and agencies.

- DeBeers: Uses the technology to track the import and sale of diamonds.

- Essentia: Uses blockchain to store passenger data in the Netherlands.

Not So Virgin

Food safety and traceability is an important topic for all countries. There is the from "farm to fork" process where food is tracked from production-> to distribution-> to retailers. For example, with blockchain technology if something is contaminated you can now destroy specific batches and not everything, which has been the normal practice.

The technology can also be unleashed to reduce fake and altered food products. The story that grabbed my attention the most was that in Europe there is more extra virgin olive oil in supply than what is actually produced. How is this possible? Because fake extra virgin olive oil is as profitable as dealing illegal narcotics, but without the risk. In a 2015 Danish food safety team random check of a 35 bottle case labelled extra virgin, only 6 were extra virgin, 12 were so bad they could not be sold to the public. One of several possible explanations, is that it all began with the distributor who certified that a supplier is "trusted." The supplier will normally provide the first few shipments as agreed, and then to increase profits they begin to slip in fakes with the future shipments.

This is not unique to Denmark or olive oil, unfortunately it happens in other countries and with other products. When I read about this case and researched further I was stunned to find out that much of the extra virgin olive oil on the market is neither extra virgin or from the country that is on the bottle label. For those that want to dive in deeper there are plenty of stories and sources on the web to follow up on.

Blockchain and Real Estate

The real estate industry is also one of the areas getting a lot of attention from blockchain specialists. Buying a home is considered a rite of passage into adulthood for many people across the globe and blockchain offers a new way to accomplish this. You can use the technology to transfer property to another party in a process that is secure, legitimate, and safe.

The current real estate market struggles with the problems of fake listings, document forgery and rental scams. The home selling process is cumbersome and is not exactly known for its speed. With smart contracts, documents and contracts are connected to a blockchain. These records are immutable, permanent and transparent. This will include an accounting system where transactions are automatically recorded and balanced without the fear of manipulation. Each individual or corporation will have a secure electronic record showing all the details. This will help to ensure that property fraud and paper deeds become things of the past.

Mini Case Study

In my research for the book, I came across a firm in the New York City area that has an innovative platform designed to service the financial sector. The platform serves as a marketplace for banks to display and sell their properties directly to homebuyers and developers. Properties are digitally sold, all initiated by smart contracts and recorded onto a private blockchain.

The platform showcases preset documents and contracts for e-signature, that minimizing the back-and-forth follow-up, and simplifies the signing process for banks and home buyers. All documents are recorded and tracked on the blockchain. Users are able to browse profiles and connect with real estate brokers, agents, lawyers, inspectors, and other professionals directly.

Similar to some famous payment systems like PayPal the platform processes online payments and transactions. The payments for real estate services and property purchases are powered by smart contracts, then recorded and tracked on their blockchain.

The users are also able to view up-to-date floor plans, property photos, 3D walk-throughs, digital videos and drone shots of the properties. They also receive a secure online wallet. They can store, receive or send digital payments to other users on the platform and yes, all payments are recorded and tracked on their private blockchain.

Obviously this is not the only firm in this sector. From my research and what anyone can confirm with a simple search on the web is that there are many firms exploring opportunities in the blockchain real estate space. I predict that of all the industries seeking practical applications of blockchain technology real estate will be one of the easiest matches.

Blockchain

as a Service (BaaS)

BaaS provides companies the opportunity to test blockchain technology without the full financial or organizational risk of developing it themselves. Organizations can evaluate the technology for their specific needs *before* adoption. Microsoft's Azure and IBM's Hyperledger are two of the best-known BaaS examples.

Developers are also busy generating their own decentralized apps on platforms such as Ethereum. Others are using the platforms to generate escrow smart contracts. These different platform options also gives developer teams opportunities to create and use their own tokens that allows them to hold ICOs.

Build Your Own Blockchain?

Ethereum allows you to create your own test blockchain network, a demo version. It is identical to the main Ethereum chain, except that transactions and smart contracts on this network are only accessible to nodes that are connected to it.

To become a node in the Ethereum network, your computer needs to download and update a copy of the entire Ethereum blockchain. They also provide the tools to download in order to interact with the network. These are, Eth and Geth.

After setting up a test blockchain, you can build smart contracts, make transactions and even distributed apps without needing real Ether. To get started, you create some fake Ether, add it to your account and then use it to make transactions.

Smart Contracts

A smart contract is a digitally enforceable contract and computer program that is stored inside of a blockchain. This is the next generation or as some describe it, the evolution of blockchains. It transforms the blockchain from a system of distributed ledgers into a new way to store, transfer, and communicate between the parts of a network.

The terms of the agreement or operation are written into lines of code which are executed when triggered by certain events. The contracts can be used to automate basic operations on a network, thus removing the need for a trusted third party.

A smart contract might allow you to send Ether on a certain date, similar to a direct payment, except that it is automated and transparent. The user creates a contract and thereafter add sufficient Ether to execute the command. Each transaction made through the contract is then recorded and updated on the blockchain.

A note: Ether is the native currency to the Ethereum blockchain.

Platform and Language

Ethereum was created and designed to support smart contracts. The Ethereum Virtual Machine (EVM) runs the contracts. This is a part of the Ethereum platform which consist of EVM, plus the Ethereum blockchain.

Solidity is the programming language used. It shares some rules and principles (syntax) of JavaScript. Ethereum has been fortunate to attract a broad community of developers and enterprises that have developed the capacity of the network by building decentralized applications.

Smart Contracts: Legally Enforceable?

Currently they are not legally enforceable, code is not law, but that might change in the future. As we know, people generally think of contracts as agreements that can be legally enforced. Smart contracts were not intended to be legally enforced. You also cannot make an illegal contract. For example a contract to commit an illegal act is not valid or enforceable.

Keep in mind, contracts require counterparties, smart contracts do not. When things do not go as planned, who do you sue? The network? The network miners? The person or team who wrote the code? Identifying a wallet address on a blockchain is not the easiest task to accomplish. A smart contract has no guarantee that you will be able to find out who used your agreement. A lawsuit must be filed against an individual. If you do not know who the other party is, then there is no case. You cannot take "no one" to court.

What happens when mistakes are in the code, leaving it open to malicious use or if transactions need to be altered or reversed? Smart contracts do not deal with ambiguity or uncertainty, which leads some cynics to complain "then they are not so smart." The reality is that programmers cannot be asked to plan for every contingency. The immutable method of enforcement also ensures that once all parties have entered a smart contract it will be carried out regardless of any other factor.

Smart Contracts: DAO

Distributed Autonomous Organization (DAO): A real-world mess. The largest smart contract to date, an investment vehicle that enabled members to participate by using their private cryptographic keys to vote on what the fund should invest in. No lawyers, no management fees. They boasted DAO "removes the ability of directors and fund managers to waste investor funds."

Due to a software bug, the DAO voted to invest $50 million of members' money into a vehicle controlled by programmers who discovered weaknesses in the software. Some said it was a hack because the software did not function as planned, others disagreed, stating that the software made decisions autonomously and if you did not understand how it worked you should not have joined.

Members watched the attackers drain the funds and they were powerless to stop it. In the end, people voted to amend the software contract and Ethereum's lead coders reversed the transaction history and returned the money to its original owners.

Smart Contracts:

The "Undo" Rule

How can we get relief after a mistake? Smart laws introduce human logic to the situation. This is a combination of current law mixed with distributed ledger technology so that justice can be done. A network can have a "undo" rule so that when executed, it is able to transfer any digital asset from one account to another. A scenario could include, that the law has a section where one member is selected and given the authority to launch the special "undo" law that freezes funds. This can be done with an algorithm. This should, in theory, reduce the incentive to steal assets since they can later be frozen and returned to the victim's account.

Another issue for members to consider is that the executor could make an error when executing the decision to freeze an account. The network then has to decide when compared to the consequences of inaction, if an error leading to the accidental stop of a contract might be the acceptable lesser of two evils.

What is an ICO?

According to a recent survey, the majority of American adults did not know what an ICO was and given the current environment that is understandable. In this chapter we will clear things up.

An Initial Coin Offering (ICO) is similar to an Initial Public Offering (IPO). In IPOs investors are asked to purchase shares of a company in the company's attempt to raise capital. However, with ICOs, investors purchase the underlying crypto tokens and they make the payment using either Bitcoin or Ether.

The first ICO was the MasterCoin Project in 2013 by J R Willet. It raised $500,000 in the form of 5,000 Bitcoins. Investors purchased MasterCoins in exchange for Bitcoins. The 5,000 Bitcoins that MasterCoin raised in 2013 was worth about $41 million in June 2018.

ICOs are popular and for now it appears that regulators remain a step behind in the action. In an attempt to catch up, several countries have placed limitations on their citizens' ability to participate. This protects people from some ICO scams but it also prevents them from getting involved in potentially profitable opportunities.

Currently, the easy money days are gone. Having just a white paper with no financial statements or evidence that the company exists and expecting that funds will roll in is a thing of the past. From 2018 on, it is more difficult to raise money, but if the project is good you are rewarded more. More funds, $9 billion was raised in the first 4 months of 2018 than all of 2017 with $6.1 billion.

USA Special Rules

Raising money through ICOs in the United States comes with some regulations specific to the US. One is Reg D 506(c), it is relatively easy and quick to comply with. There is no cap on the amount that you can raise; you file a form D. The downside is that you are limited to raising money from accredited investors. An accredited investor is a person that earns at least $200,000 per year or has at least a million US Dollars in assets outside of their primary residence.

The other regulation is Reg A, you can raise up to $50 million, you can solicit or market the deal, and anyone over 18 globally can invest. It is costly and time-consuming and it also requires filing with the SEC, plus 2 years of audited financials.

Both of these regulations have led to some projects bypassing the United States in favor of other countries with more relaxed rules.

Comparing ICOs with Traditional Funding

ICOs globally are mostly unregulated. In the US, the Securities and Exchange Commission (SEC) has reacted and considers many of them as securities. ICOs pass the Howey test and this means that security regulations apply.

In traditional funding, you pay to own a percentage of a company. The percentage owned is constant and so is the dollar amount that you paid. To launch an IPO, a company needs to satisfy a list of requirements that includes earnings threshold, verification of accounts, minimum market capitalization, etc.

In the world of ICOs the owners can raise funds without cumbersome shareholder agreements. When they get Bitcoin or Ether, the company does not give up equity in exchange for the investment that was made. You only invest in the development of a firm's technology or project but not in the firm. To be very clear, you have no ownership stake in the firm itself.

The dollar value of the Bitcoin or Ether received in the exchange can increase and obviously it can also go down. For example, an ICO raises $5 million of Bitcoins in September, the amount raised can be worth $8 million in December.

Token Evolution

A token is launched through an ICO. They are issued to investors in exchange for either Bitcoin or Ether. After the ICO, the public can buy, sell, or hold the tokens in the same way they can with a stock. Investors hope that the tokens will increase in enough value that they will be able to cash out with a profit.

Ethereum technology provides the base on which tokens are built. It is the market leader for tokens (for now). There are currently over 70,000 tokens on the Ethereum network. For the adventurous ones there are several sites that even allow you to create your own.

Tokens can represent anything from real commodities to currencies used in blockchain ecosystems. Bottom line, a coin does one thing and programmable tokens can fulfil many types of functions.

ERC20

ERC20 (Ethereum Request for Comment), is the guideline followed when creating tokens. It standardizes token smart contracts by eliminating the need for exchanges and wallets to create a custom code for each token. ERC20 tokens are used by most ICOs.

Currency Tokens

The original currency token is Bitcoin and it is still the leader. Currency tokens are designed to be digital cash: They are used in the exchange of goods and services or traded on the market. They are not legal tender as yet but let us see how their stories unfold. Their values are based mostly on speculation and the usual conditions of supply and demand.

Utility Tokens

Ethereum was the first major utility token and it also does duty as a currency token. Utility tokens allows you to do things. This, for example, can take the form of running smart contracts on the blockchain. Utility tokens are sometimes referred to as Network Access Tokens. They give you access to something a network offers.

Asset Tokens

They represent some sort of asset or product. The tokens can also represent ownership or the right of use. There is the risk that if the underlying asset depreciates, so does the token. The obvious goal is to tokenize things that are expected to increase in value and it could even include traditional assets like gold.

Equity Tokens

Like a stock, an equity token buys a degree of ownership of an organization. An equity token implies ownership and control. The Ethereum based DAO was the first major equity token. Owners of DAO tokens had control over the activities of the organization.

The rules of what is an equity can be unclear depending on whom you speak to. I suggest that you consult a lawyer. If the token provides you a reward or benefit off the actions of others, or if the token involves making money exclusively off the actions of others, it might be an equity (this brings regulations).

Reputation and Reward Tokens

These are given as symbols of reputation or rewards. They are a way of specifying on a blockchain that some user or wallet did something special or is someone special.
The value of a reputation token is that you can trust that the person in possession of one is who they say they are.

Security Token Offerings?

Security Token Offerings (STOs) are regulated offerings in which the issuer sells programmable equity to investors. STOs come with additional complexity that includes lots of paperwork, lawyers, underwriting, and regulations. STOs are often seen as more stable and legitimate than some ICOs, as they can provide investors upfront reassurance that they are less likely to run into problems later.

The Latest in Token Evolution (FYI)

ERC721: Has been adopted as the standard token for deploying digital art or unique collectibles on the blockchain and blockchain gaming apps.

ERC1155: The latest token entering the blockchain gaming world. Both are non-fungible, each token is unique.

Token Evolution (ERC20 FYI)

This is a little extra for those that want to know the guidelines that must be followed for ERC20 tokens creation.

Total Supply: defines the total supply of tokens. When this limit is reached the smart contract stops issuing more tokens.

Balance of: indicates how many tokens a given address has.

Transfer: takes a certain amount of tokens from the total supply and gives to a user.

Transfer From: can be used to transfer tokens between any two users that have them.

Approve: verifies that your contract can give a certain amount of tokens to a user.

Allowance: checks if a user has enough balance to send a certain amount to tokens to another user.

ICO Ratings, Can You Trust Them?

Ratings are important because inexperienced investors are especially trusting of ICO rating platforms when seeking information before investing. The reality is that rating platforms have always been looked at with suspicion among more experienced market players. To begin, it is relatively easy to buy ICO ratings, therefore ratings on ICO sites in many, many cases are not independent.

"ICO ratings from a trusted source"is a version of what ICO rating platforms advertise on their websites to gain the trust of investors looking for information. A nice claim, but investigations of the websites showed that an ICO rating's visibility is not always impartial. The results are frightening, the players basically "pay to play."

Many platforms are nothing more than marketing sites selling to the highest bidders.

They offer prime listing services in exchange for payment. ICOs can secure a top tier ranking in an ICO overview and be featured in special mailings. If the ICO is willing to pay up, the site can block their competitors from appearing on the profile pages of the paying ICO. These paid top listings are not labelled as sponsored.

If you already have a rating that is not that high, it is not unheard of to be contacted by services offering to boost it. Keep in mind inexperienced investors use this information to make investment decisions which is a serious problem.

What is Next for Blockchains?

Directed Acyclic Graphs (DAGs)

Directed Acyclic Graphs are not completely new, in 2015 the first proposal was introduced to mix it with blockchain technology. Sergio Lerner introduced the idea with a project that he was working on, the project failed, but it opened the door for developers to expand upon the DAG concept. DAGs are not blockchains, there is no chain which links all the blocks. There are no blocks at all and the transactions on individual nodes do not need to be synchronized with any other. This allows transactions to occur without the confirmation of the entire network, significantly reducing the normal confirmation time.

How do DAGs Work?

On a DAG there is no need for miner rewards and there are no transaction fees for the end user. Transactions are confirmed through a process where a user confirms two previous transactions in order for their own transactions to be processed.

Every transaction acts as its own block, and these can be stored in different locations, on multiple devices, before syncing up with a node somewhere on the graph. The syncing process updates the ledger with the final transaction details of all the interactions that took place among the addresses on the graph.

IOTA is probably the most well-known adopter of DAG technology. They refer to it as the Tangle. Tangle is the web that makes up IOTA's network of users who serve as both transactors and verifiers at the same time. To issue a transaction, users must work to approve other transactions. The assumption is the nodes will insure that the approved transactions are not conflicting and will not approve those that do. As a transaction gets more approvals, it becomes more accepted by the system.

All technology comes with its weak points. DAG coins claim to be quantum-resistant, but there is uncertainty about their ability to survive a 33% attack. This is the amount of computing power necessary to attack and take over a Proof-of-Stake DAG network.

There are also concerns over the ability for DAG networks to be fully decentralized. Since validations by all nodes on the network is not required, there are more opportunities for misconduct, the main one being double spend. To protect against this scenario, many DAG projects have coordinator nodes. This brings a centralized element and ensures a linear order of transactions within the DAG. The IOTA developers run their own coordinator node at all times in order to protect the network.

The concerns of centralization that exist with DAGs also exist with Bitcoin and other cryptos that can be heavily influenced by a small number of large traders known as whales.

Blockchain
First Aid Kit

This chapter has the blockchain "first aid" kit. These are the terms and concepts that I believe are essential to know in addition to the content from the previous chapters. The "kit" has the terms conveniently compiled by sections for you. Study them and you will noticeably improve your understanding of blockchain technology.

Double-spending: a potential flaw in cryptos is the risk that a digital currency can be spent twice. This is possible because a token consists of a digital file that can be duplicated or falsified. Cryptographic techniques are used to prevent double-spending while preserving anonymity.

Fungibility: is the property of a good or a commodity whose individual units are interchangeable. For example, one kilo of pure gold is equivalent to any other kilo of pure gold, whether in the form of coins or in other states, gold is fungible. Other fungible examples include, crude oil, shares, bonds, currencies. A diamond is not, since each is unique.

EOS: allows developers to create blockchain applications. Scalable and programmable, EOS has been called 'Ethereum on Steroids'. The EOS blockchain eliminates transaction fees and has the ability to process millions of transactions a second.

Casper + Sharding: the significant change coming to Ethereum over the next years is the proposal to switch from Proof-of-Work to Proof-of-Stake (as part of Casper), and break up the network into a bunch of partitions called shards. Each shard would have an independent state and transaction history. Validators on the network wouldn't be responsible for handling all transactions; instead, notaries within each shard would be responsible for their own shard.

Ethereum Viper: is a project created by Ethereum. It is an experimental programming language. It is an alternative way to build projects for the Ethereum ecosystem in the future. For now, coding with Solidity remains the primary programming language for the ecosystem.

MakerDAO: is one of the most prominent Decentralized Autonomous Organizations (DAOs) built on the Ethereum blockchain. One of their core products is the DAI stablecoin, which is a crypto-collateralized stablecoin.

Quantum Computing: as of 2018, the development of actual quantum computers is still in its infancy. Large-scale quantum computers would theoretically be able to solve certain problems significantly faster than regular computers. A quantum computer could efficiently break many of the security systems in use today. These systems are used to protect encrypted emails, secure web pages, and many other types of data. Breaking these would have significant consequences for electronic security.

Hashing: when a user sends a secure message, a hash of the intended message is generated and encrypted, and is sent along with the message. When the message is received, the receiver decrypts the hash as well as the message. Then, the receiver creates another hash from the message. If the two hashes are identical when compared, then a secure transmission has occurred. This hashing process ensures that the message is not altered by an unauthorized end user.

Quorum Blockchain: developed by J.P. Morgan, Quorum is one of the first major steps towards common adoption of blockchain among financial industries. Quorum is a permissioned blockchain infrastructure specifically designed for financial use cases.

Cardano Blockchain: similar to Ethereum, Cardano is a smart contract platform however, Cardano offers more scalability.

Dapps: Decentralized Apps. Dapps work in synergy with smart contracts and perform the role of an automated middleman. In the world of contracts when an agreement is reached, the broker ensures that the terms of the agreement are honored. A Dapp performs the same function using the blockchain to replace the broker.

DAUs: Daily Active Users

DADs: Daily Active Developers

Stablecoins: are cryptocurrencies that attempt to maintain a stable price; most attempt to peg their price to 1 US Dollar, but they could theoretically attempt a peg to anything, such as a basket of goods. A good number of people in the crypto community are skeptical that they will work.

Airdrops

Airdrop: airdrop is the process where a cryptocurrency team distributes cryptocurrency tokens to the wallets of some users for free. Airdrops are usually carried out by blockchain startups to boost their projects.

Reasons for an Airdrop:

To Reward Loyal Customers: blockchain services like cryptocurrency exchanges, trading platforms, wallet service providers, etc. wish to reward their customers and subscribers. This serves as an incentive that can help to keep clients loyal.

To Expand a Lead Database: airdrops can be used by blockchain firms to generate a valuable database of leads for their growing organizations. In exchange for free cryptocurrency tokens, users will be asked to complete online forms that contain valuable user information (email addresses) which can be used to develop marketing campaigns.

To Get the Word Out About a New Crypto: a new cryptocurrency can go completely unnoticed if it isn't given the right boost in terms of substantial marketing campaigns. With cryptocurrency enthusiasts looking for new cryptocurrency options, an airdrop is a way to get people interested in a new crypto.

Consensus Methods:

Proof-of-Work: is the first and most widely used method of establishing consensus. Proof-of-Work consensus is where each node is required to complete an extremely complex equation in order to finish each block.

The purpose of the complexity of the equation is to ensure that each node is forced to exert a significant amount of processing power and electricity in order to solve it. In return for solving the block, each node is given a block reward that typically comes in the form of cryptocurrency in addition to the transaction fees. This process is referred to as mining, and the nodes that choose to do it are called miners. In order to regulate this consensus system, if a miner gets a different answer than the other miners working on the same block, their answer is rejected. Miners don't want to use processing power and electricity without a reward, so they are economically incentivized to provide correct answers.

In a Proof-of-Work system, the only way to cheat is to control more than 51% of the ledgers, which is the same as possessing more than 51% of the total processing power dedicated to the platform. Even with this advantage, it would be extremely difficult to alter past transactions, and practically impossible to change transactions further than several blocks.

A miner that controls more than 51% of the processing power would have the ability to not only prevent transactions from executing and but also reverse transactions. This level of control would require a huge amount of capital (estimates are in the range of half a billion US Dollars), therefore it does not make much economic sense for a miner to attempt this kind of scheme.

The more processing power a miner has access to, the more likely it is that they will be able to correctly solve the solution to the complex equation first before other miners and win the block reward. A common practice has developed in which many miners join together and combine their processing power into a "mining pool." With this method, miners are usually able to generate a consistent income as opposed to sporadic and unpredictable income.

In mining terms, block difficulty refers to how difficult the equation for each block is to solve. If the blocks are being solved too slowly, then the block difficulty is reduced. If blocks are being solved too rapidly, the block difficulty is increased.

Good:

- Proof-of-Work consensus is capital intensive, and requires node operators to be heavily invested in the cryptocurrency that they are mining. This also functions as an economic measure against cheating.
- The potential profits that mining offers leads to the creation of more nodes, this has the effect of increasing the total computing power, improving the security of the network

The not so good:

- Proof-of-Work consensus uses a huge amount of energy. For comparison, one transaction using PoW consensus uses the similar amount of energy that an average household uses in a 24 hour period.
- PoW consensus typically has slower transaction confirmation times than other consensus methods

Examples of PoW Cryptocurrencies:

- Bitcoin
- Litecoin
- Bitcoin Cash

Proof-of-Stake (PoS): is a consensus method in which there are no miners. Instead, nodes are merely selected for the processing of transactions without needing to compute and solve complex equations. Other nodes in a Proof-of-Stake system will verify the block. In order to prevent cheating, nodes in a Proof-of-Stake system must lock a specific amount of currency in a virtual safe. This currency is forfeited as a penalty if any irregularities are detected. This process is known as Staking, and can be considered to function in a similar way as mining in Proof-of-Work systems but without the huge energy expenditure. The more currency that is staked by a node, the higher the chance that it will be selected to create the next block. This also means that nodes that attempt to cheat the system have more to lose in the process.

Good:

- PoS offers quicker confirmation times than PoW
- Proof-of-Stake executes more transactions per second than Proof-of-Work platforms

The not so good:

- There are remains a number of unanswered questions surrounding the security of Proof-of-Stake systems

Examples of PoS Cryptocurrencies:

- Peercoin

- Ethereum

Proof-of-Importance (PoI): users are obligated to provide as collateral a fixed amount of currency in order to become a node. The chances that they will be the node chosen to create a block and claim the fees depends on their importance score. The importance score of a node in PoI is determined by how frequently they use and add to the network. Nodes that send a huge amount of currency are often ranked with the highest importance scores.

Good:

- Proof-of-Importance consensus encourages the use of a cryptocurrency as a currency
- PoI rewards users that are heavily invested in the currency
- The Proof-of-Importance method appears to be secure and efficient
- Easily scalable

The not so good:

- The complex method used to determine the importance score has the potential to turn away new investors

Examples of PoI Cryptocurrencies:

- NEM

Delegated Byzantine Fault Tolerance (dBFT): in Delegated Byzantine Fault Tolerance, nodes are established by delegated shareholders. In order for a node to be elected, they are required to stake some of their currency. In Delegated Byzantine Fault Tolerance nodes are weighted equally.

A minimum amount of currency must be used as collateral for every node a user wishes to control. This makes it expensive to control more nodes, and more unlikely that any of these extra nodes will be elected. In dBFT consensus, shareholders are more likely to elect nodes that offer the lower transaction fees.

This democratic consensus technique both promotes usage of the network and lowers usage fees. The low transaction fees generated by dBFT reduces the overall profit profile offered by becoming a node, preventing potential abusers from achieving massive profits by establishing node pools. There is no mining in the Delegated Byzantine Fault Tolerance method. Financial benefits are provided in the form of transaction fees paid to nodes.

Good:

- Very quick confirmation times
- dBFT offers high transaction per second capacity
- Very low transaction fees- dBFT is currently transaction fee free

The not so good:

- The dBFT technique has not been tested at a large scale

Examples of dBFT Cryptocurrencies:

- NEO

Tangle: is technically not a blockchain. The Tangle consensus method utilizes a system that relies on every user of the network functioning as a node. Before a user can confirm a transaction, the user is required to validate two or more other transactions.

After the user has validated two previous transactions, a second user will validate the first transaction as part of their own transaction process. In this sense, the Tangle consensus method is closer to a net of transactions, in comparison to a blockchain with its chain of blocks.

The structure of Tangle provides users with free and instant transactions, and this scales well. There remains several questions regarding security and there is the issue that the entire network still requires super-nodes that moderate and oversee the network.

Good:

- Instant transactions
- Free transactions
- The low computational power demands by Tangle consensus makes it adequate for devices with low processing capacity, such as smartphones

The not so good:

- Tangle currently appears to be less secure than other consensus methods
- The Tangle network uses a Coordinator, which can be considered to function like a supervisor that guides the network until it is large enough to function autonomously. There is uncertainty regarding how efficiently the Tangle network will operate once the Coordinator is disabled.

Examples of Tangle Cryptocurrencies:

- IOTA

Conclusion

Thank you for making it through to the end of *The Cryptocurrency-Blockchain Connection.* Let's hope it was informative and that the pages were able to provide you with the knowledge needed to achieve the goal of expanding your understanding of cryptocurrencies and blockchains. The next step, as I always recommend in my books is to take action by reading more or even taking one of my courses.

Profile of The Author

Wayne Walker is the director of a global capital markets education and consulting firm (gcmsonline.info). He has several years experience in leading and coaching teams of Investment Advisors and has managed top performing teams in the Private Client Group based on Bench Mark Earnings (BME).

www.ingramcontent.com/pod-product-compliance
Lightning Source LLC
Chambersburg PA
CBHW031224050326
40689CB00009B/1468